TIM JEFFS ART
Animal Sketches
Lizards

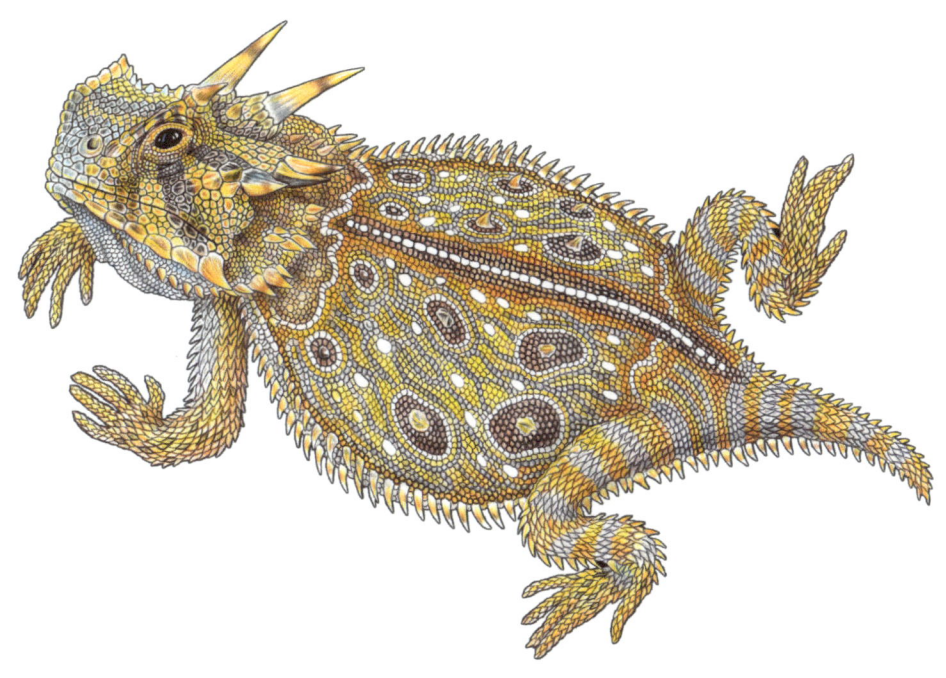

Coloring Book

Lizard Thoughts

Thousands and thousands of scales. The ornate scales that adorn lizards have always been a favorite drawing subject of mine. It was an intricate drawing of a chameleon that led me down the path of creating coloring books. And from that drawing on I have done numerous drawing of all kinds of lizards. This coloring book brings together many of the lizards I have drawn over the years. From colorful chameleons to the largest lizard, the Komodo Dragon, this compilation of 20 drawings will excite any reptile enthusiast to pick up a coloring pencil and have fun!

Tim Jeffs
Wildlife Artist

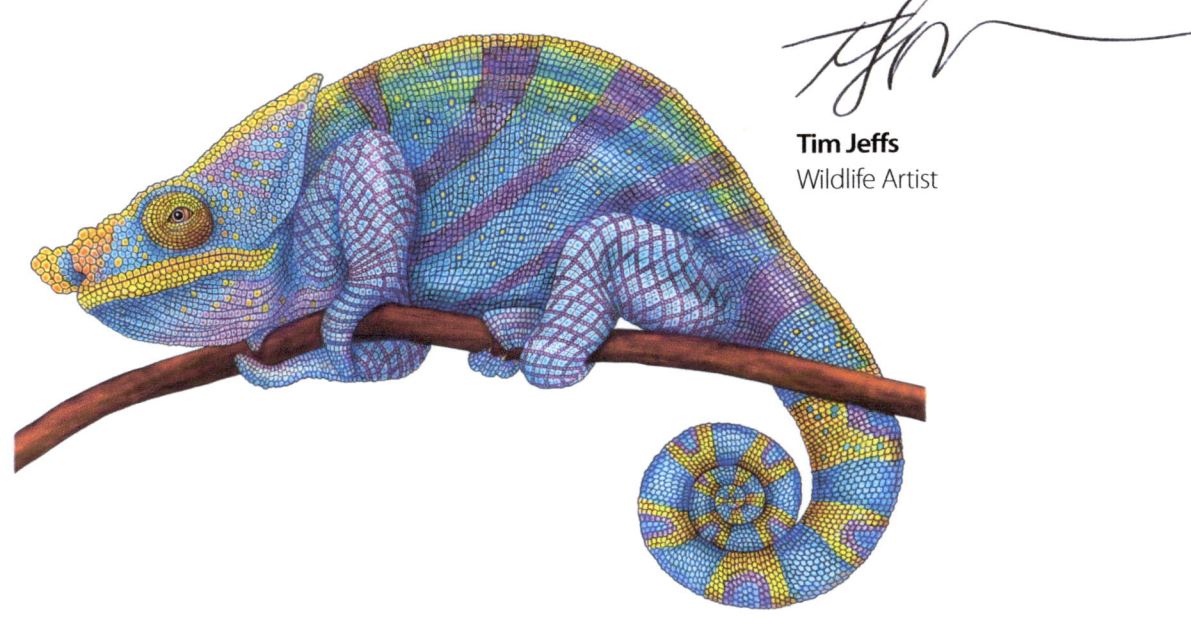

For Jane, Jenna and Harrison

Dedicated to all of the wonderful colorists who have supported my art and made my drawings more beautiful with their colors, and all the precious creatures that we live among.

A special thank you to Jo Warren and Karl Jennings for all of their continued support.

© Copyright 2021 Tim Jeffs Art

All rights reserved. No part of this publication may be reproduced or distributed in any form without the prior written permission of Tim Jeffs Art.

Tim Jeffs Art

376 East Madison Avenue, Dumont, NJ 07628

Lizard Index

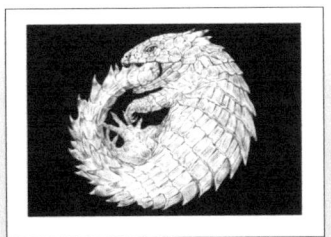
Armadillo Girdled Lizard 1

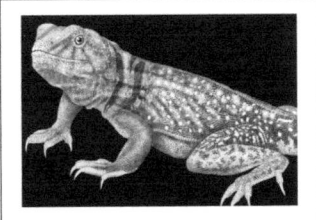
Collared Lizard 5

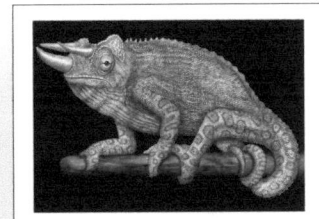
Jackson's Chameleon 9

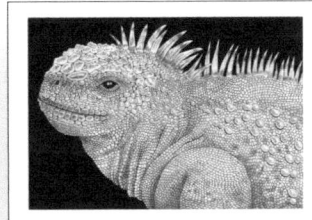
Marine Iguana 13

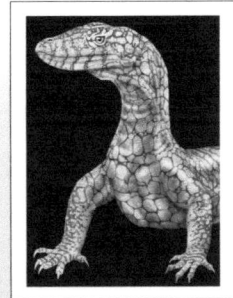
Perentie 17

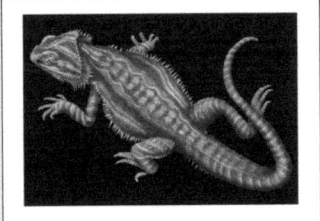
Bearded Dragon 2

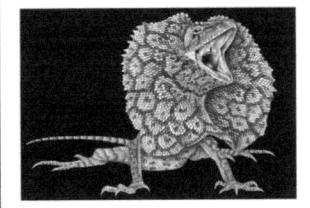
Frilled Neck Lizard 6

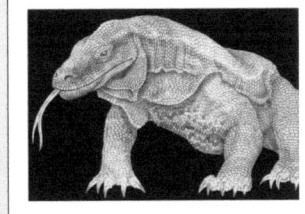
Komodo Dragon 10

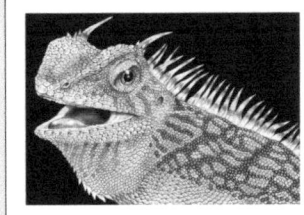
Mountain Horned Lizard 14

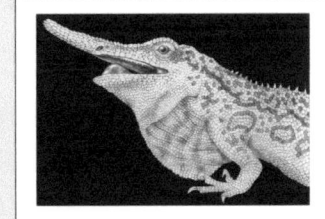
Pinocchio Lizard 18

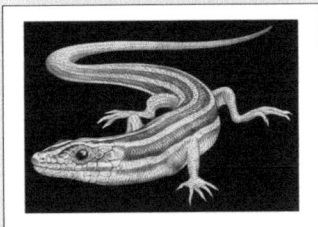
Blue-Tailed Skink 3

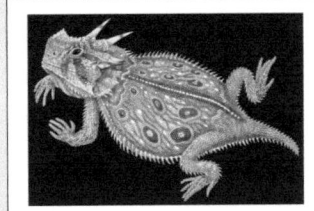
Horned Lizard 7

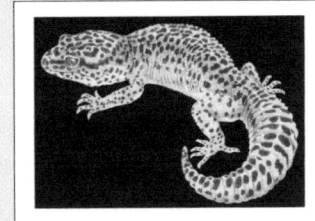
Leopard Gecko 11

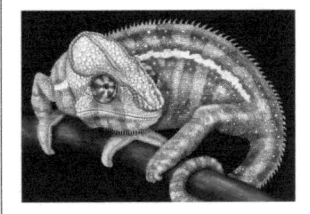
Panther Chameleon 15

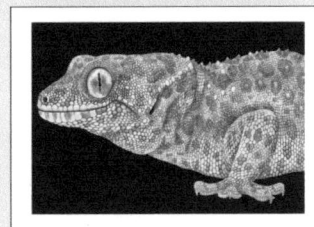
Tokay Gecko 19

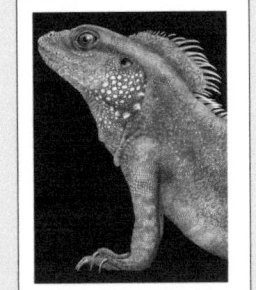
Chinese Water Dragon 4

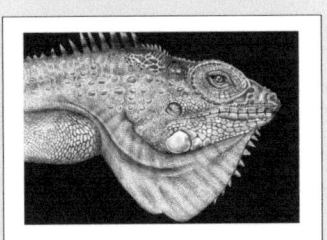
Iguana 8

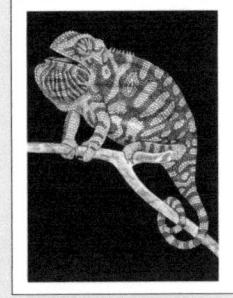
Lesser Chameleon 12

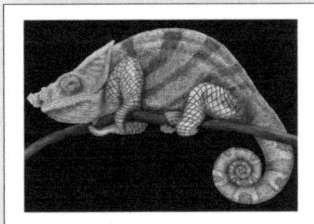
Parsons Chameleon 16

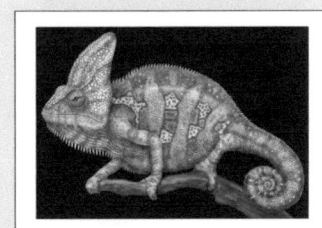
Veiled Chameleon 20

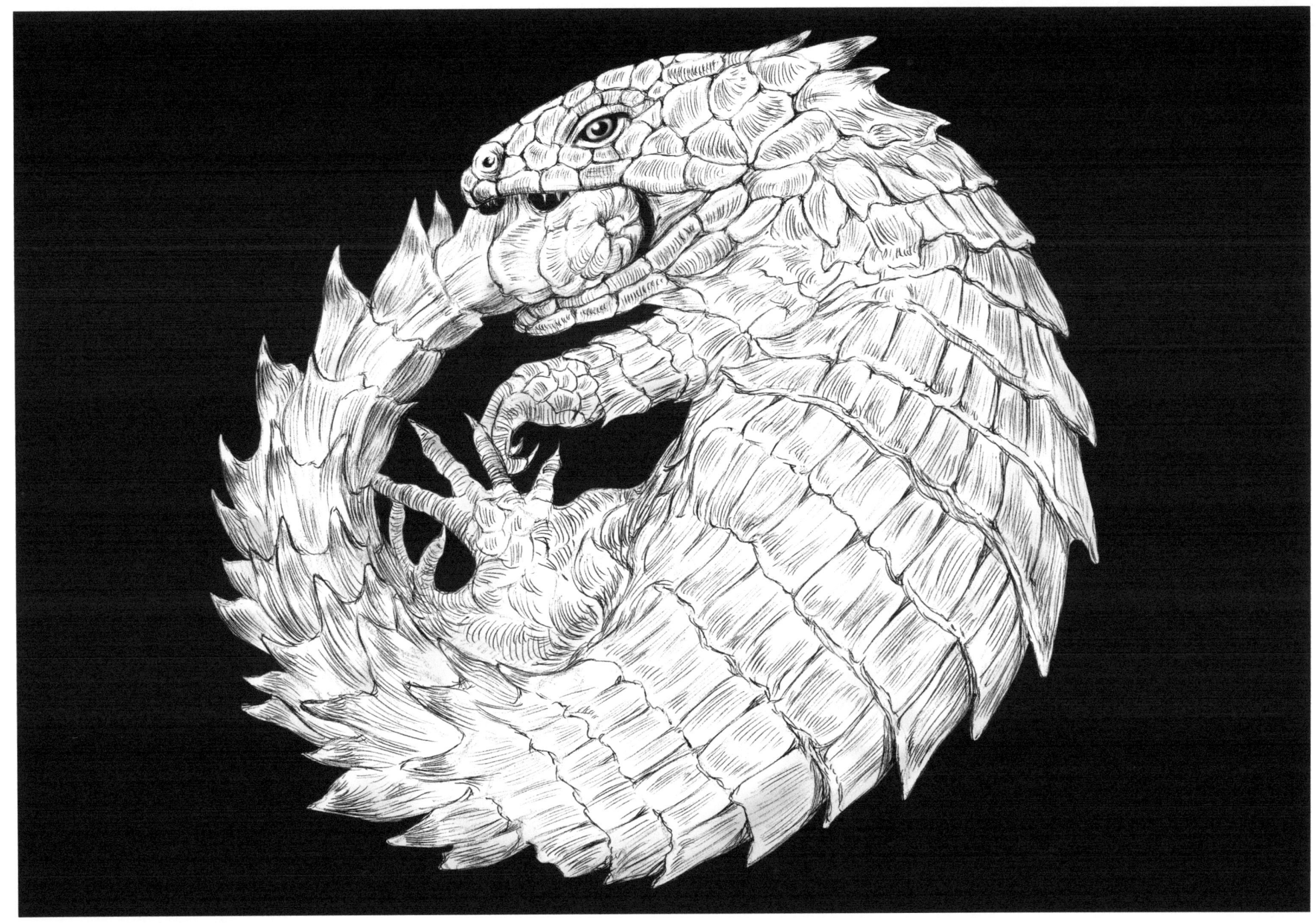

Armadillo Girdled Lizard

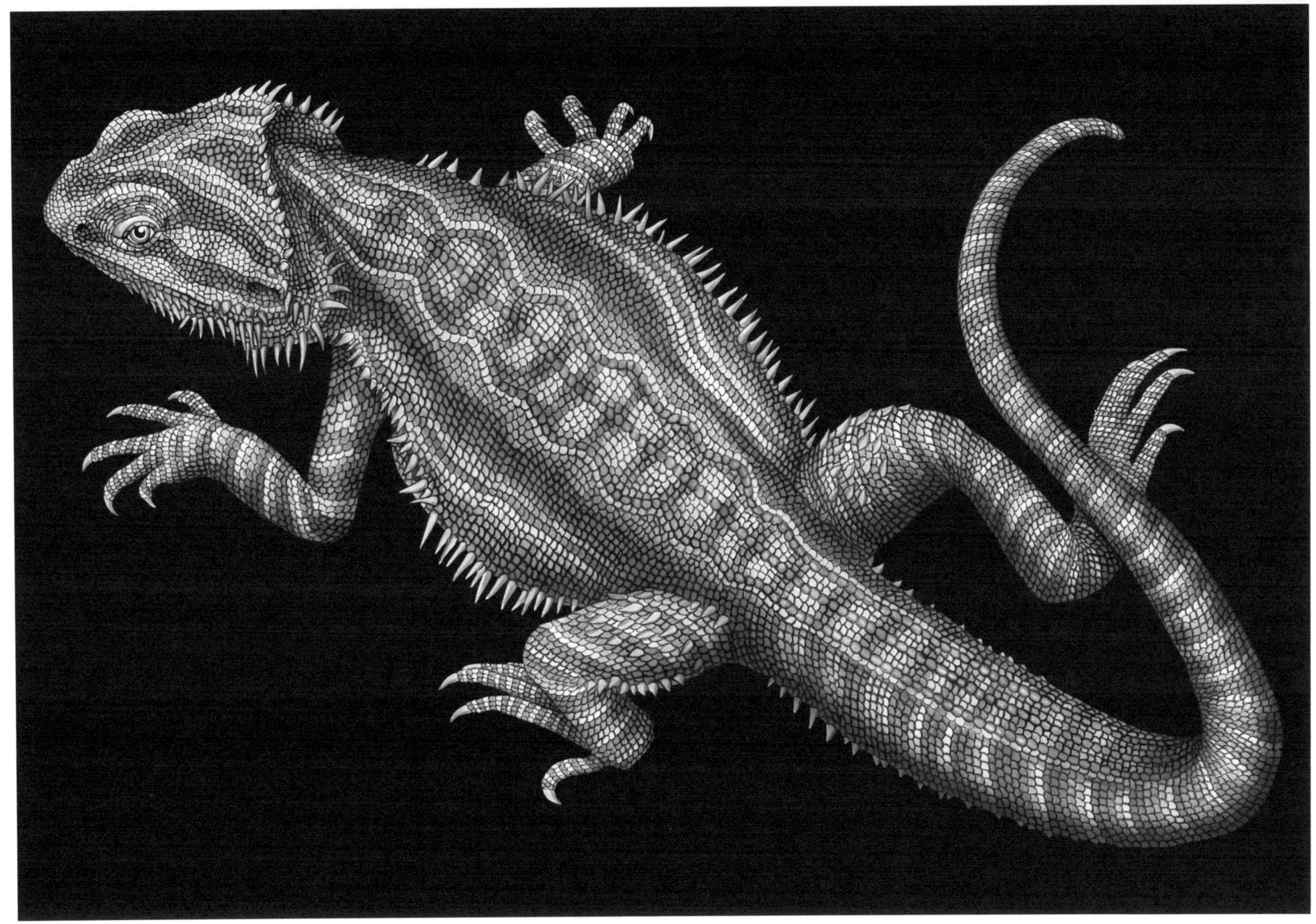

Bearded Dragon

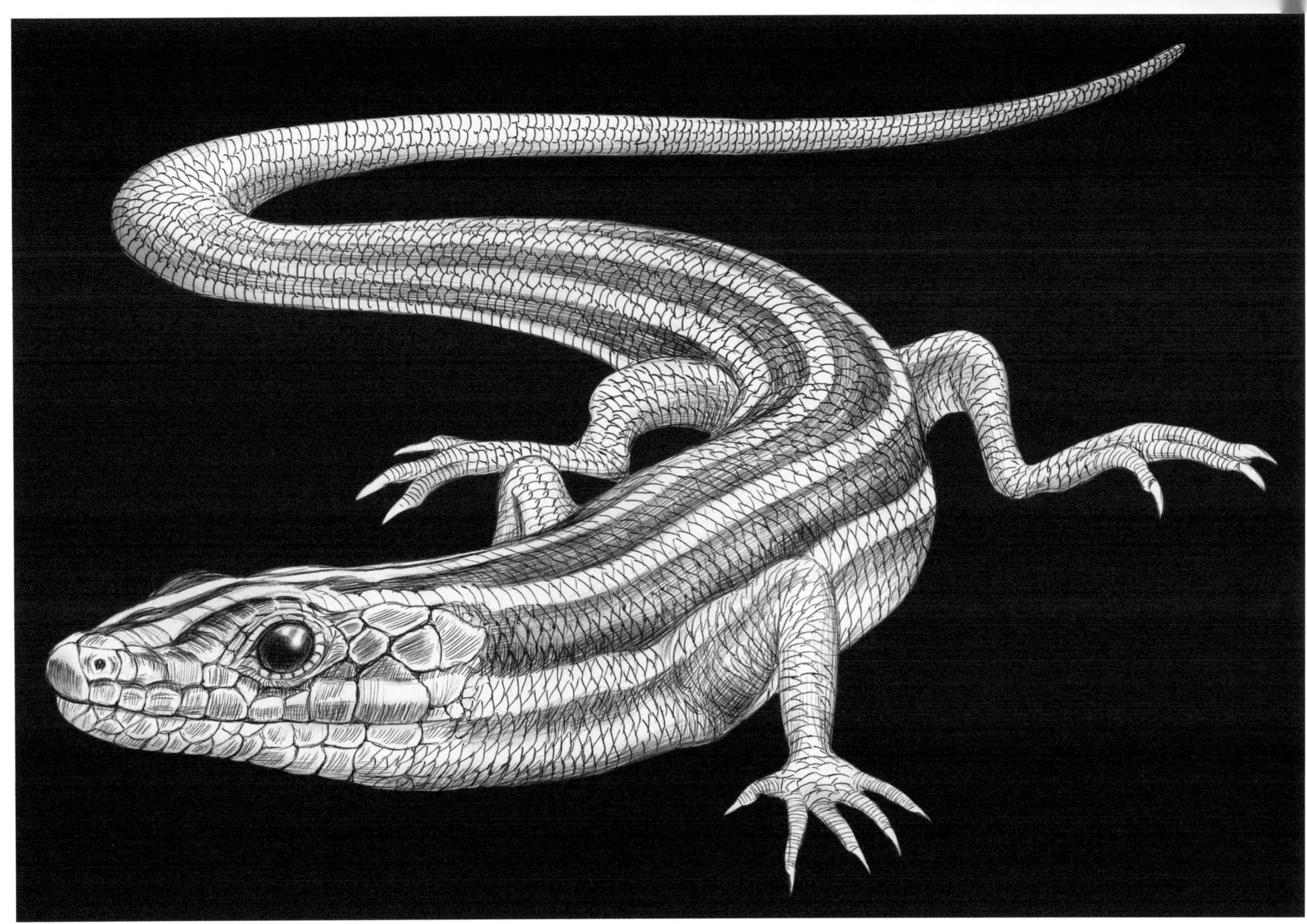

Blue-Tailed Skink

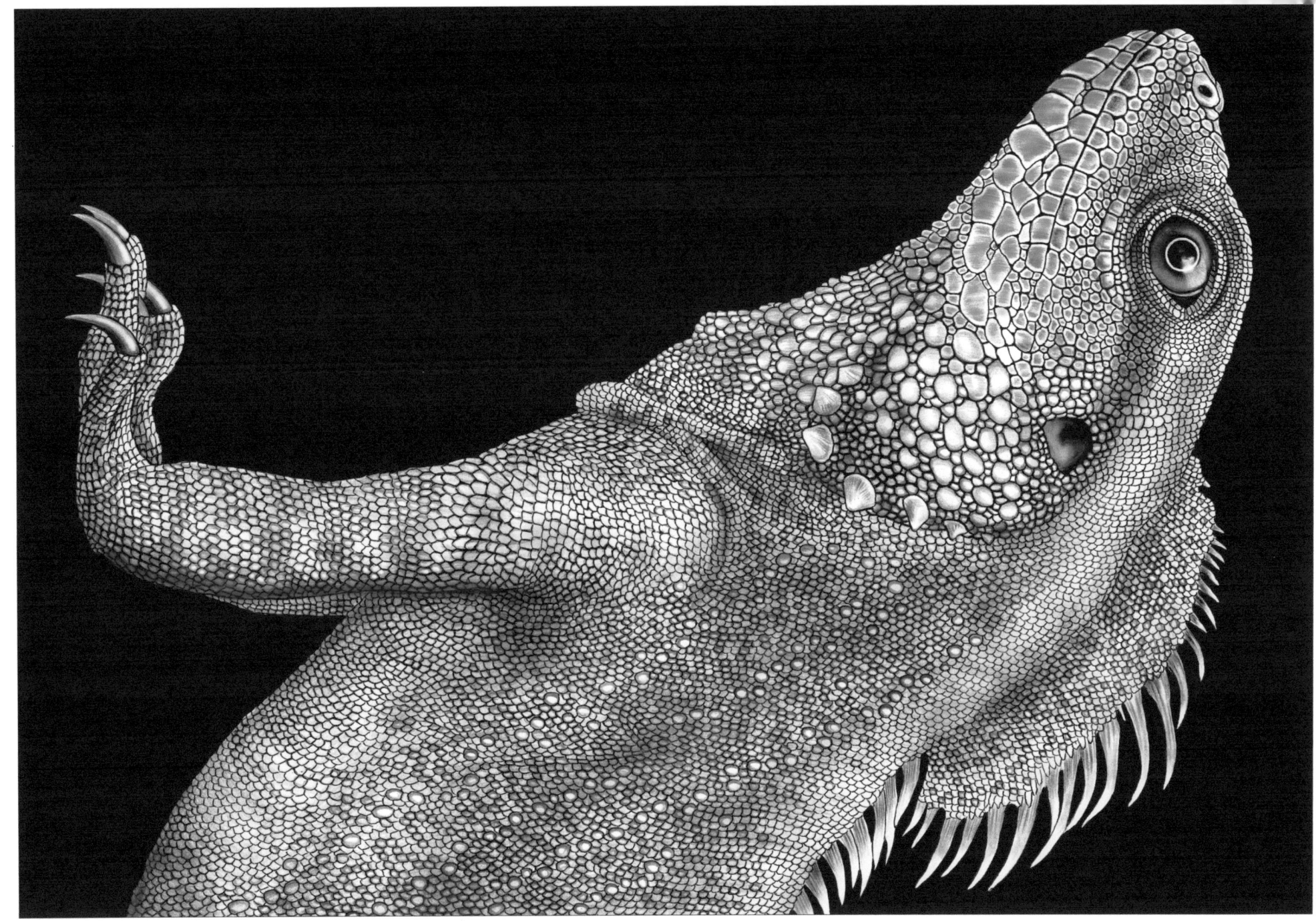

Chinese Water Dragon

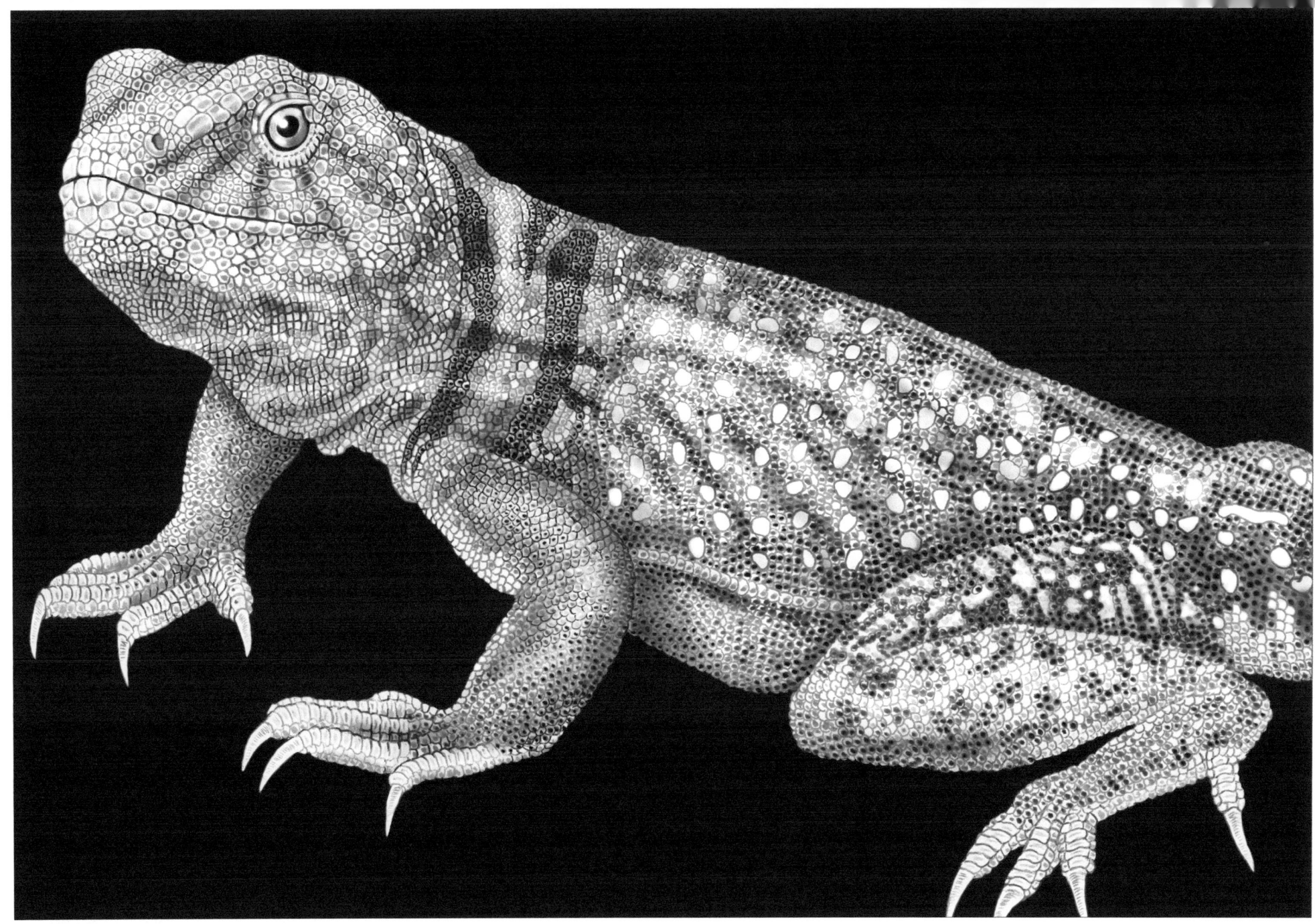

Collared Lizard

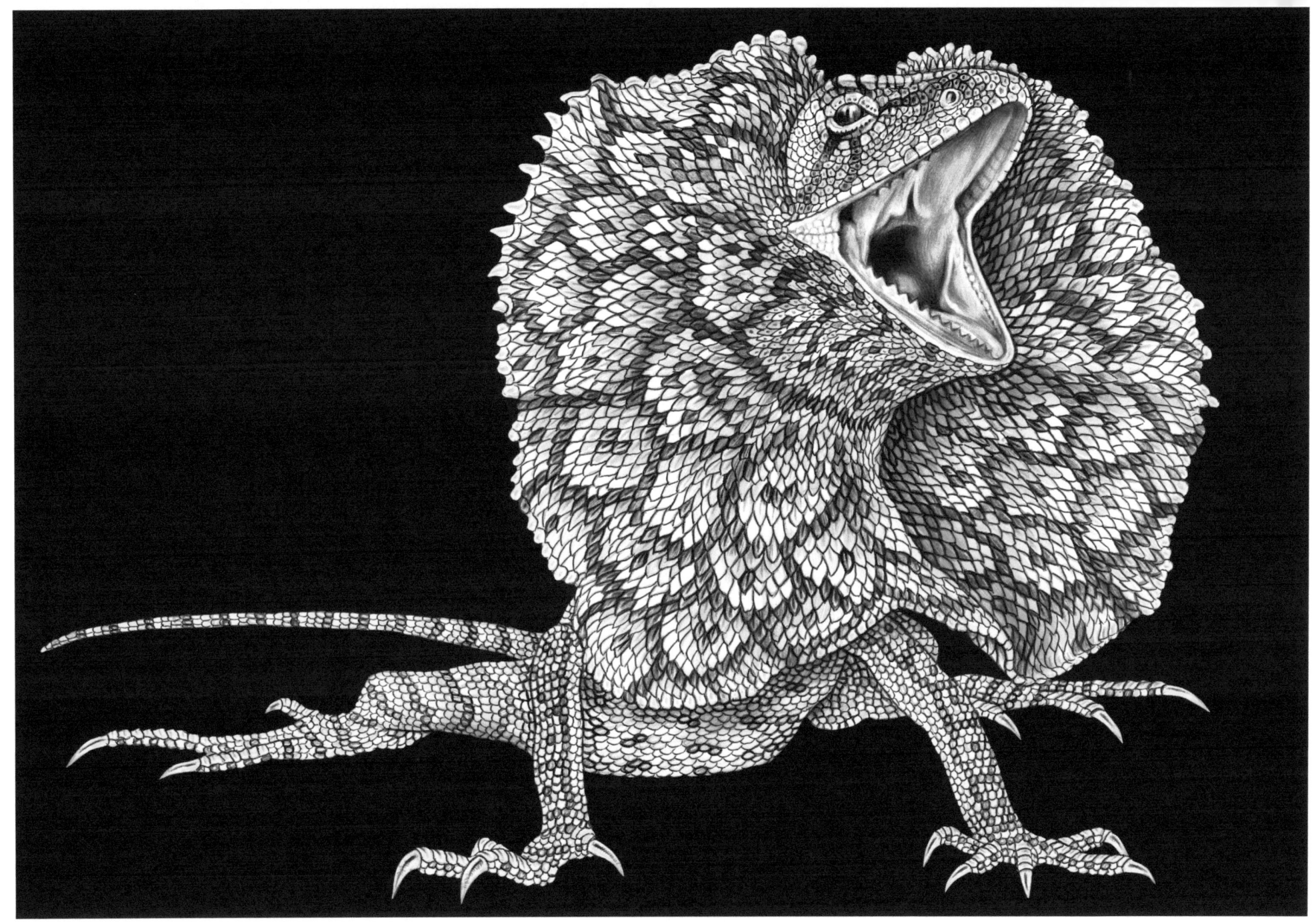

Frilled Neck Lizard

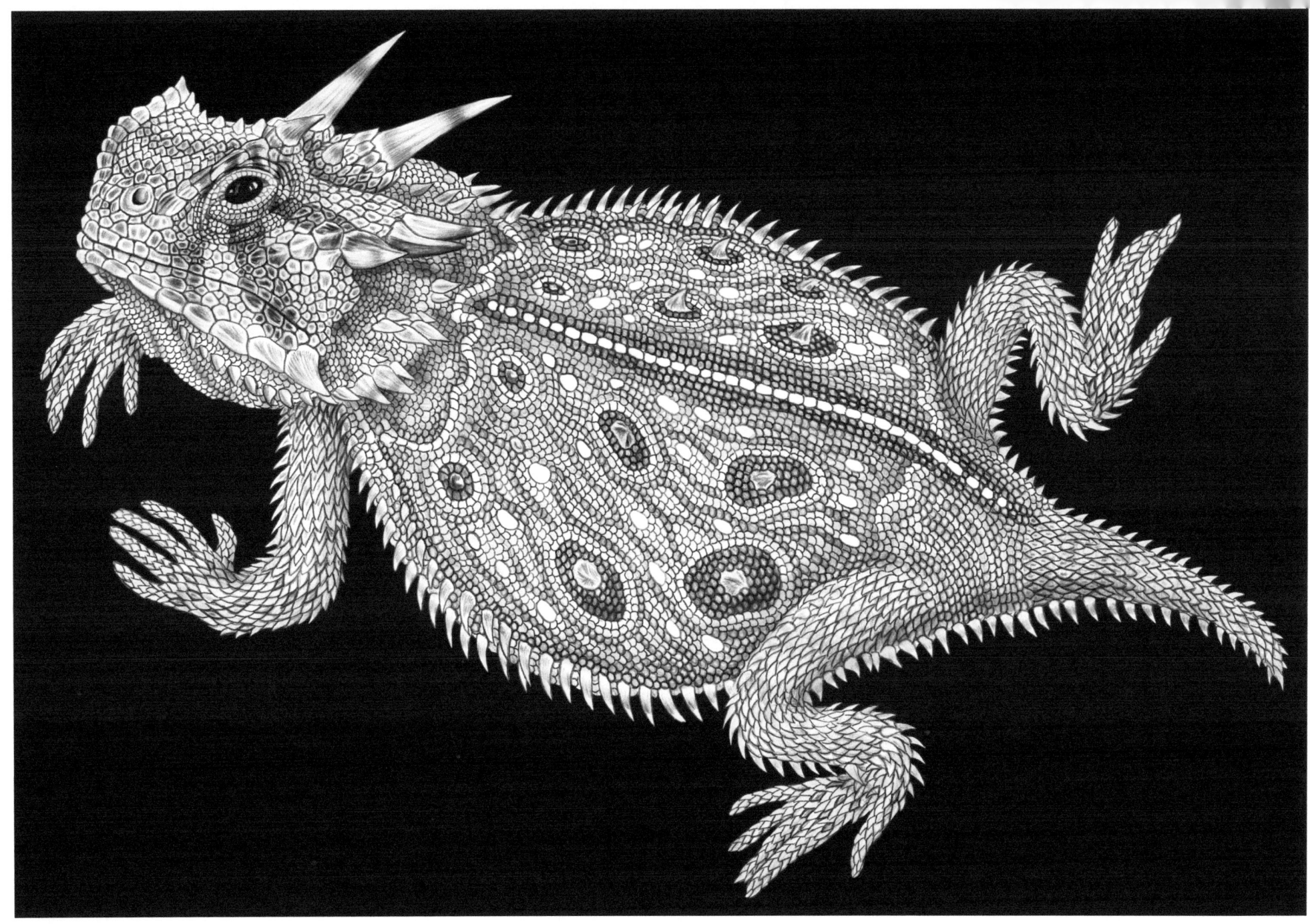

Horned Lizard

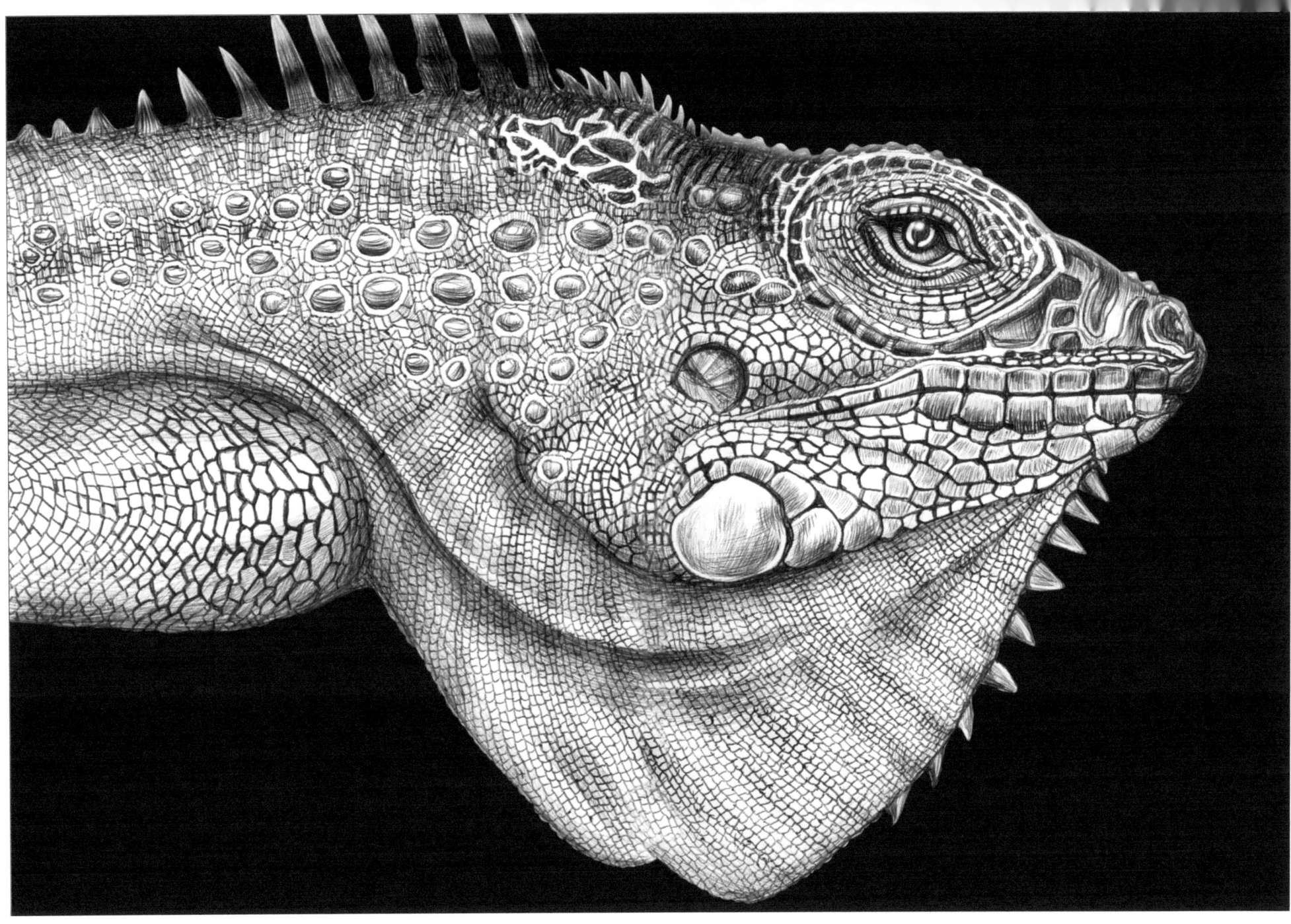

Iguana

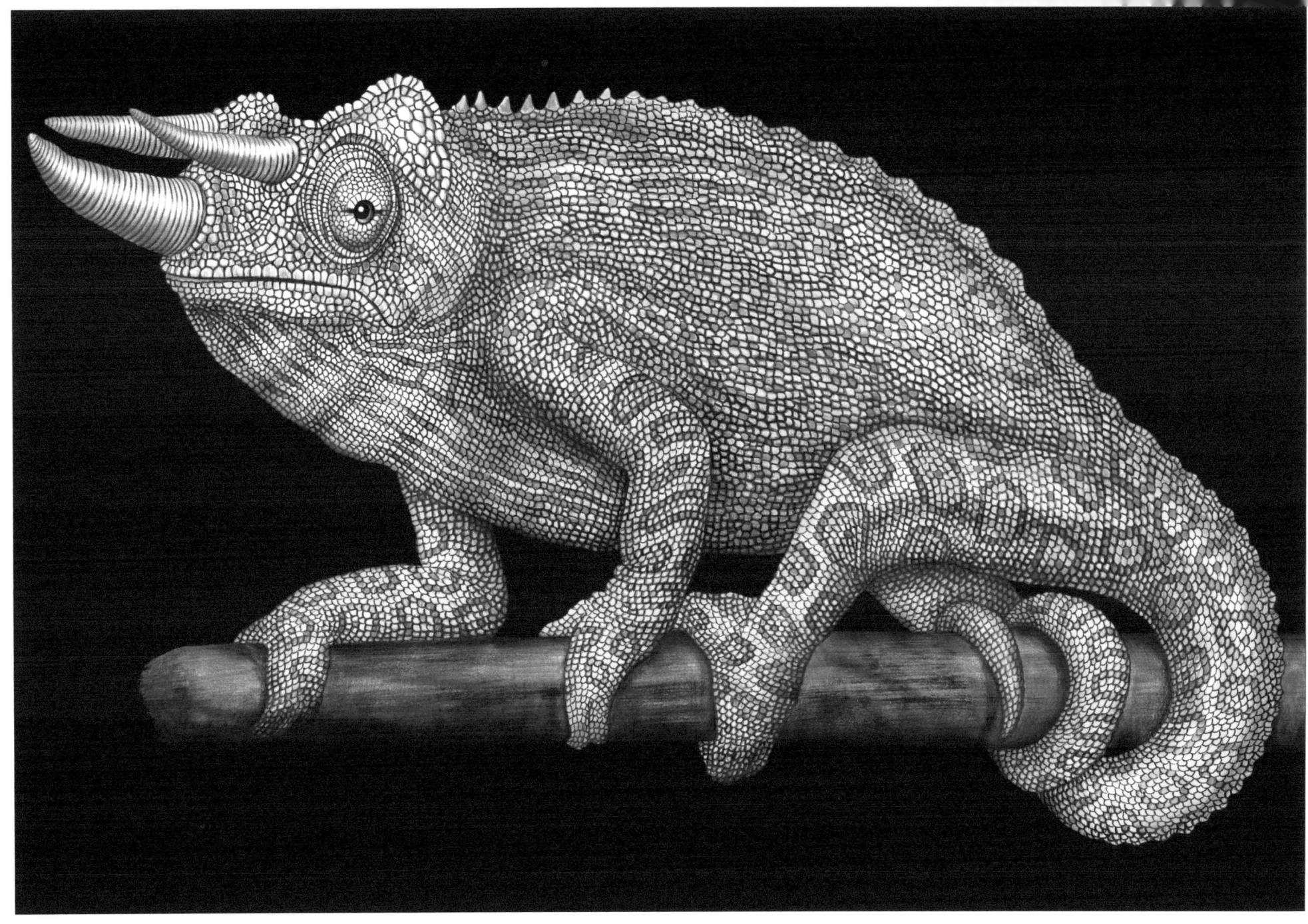

Jackson's Chameleon

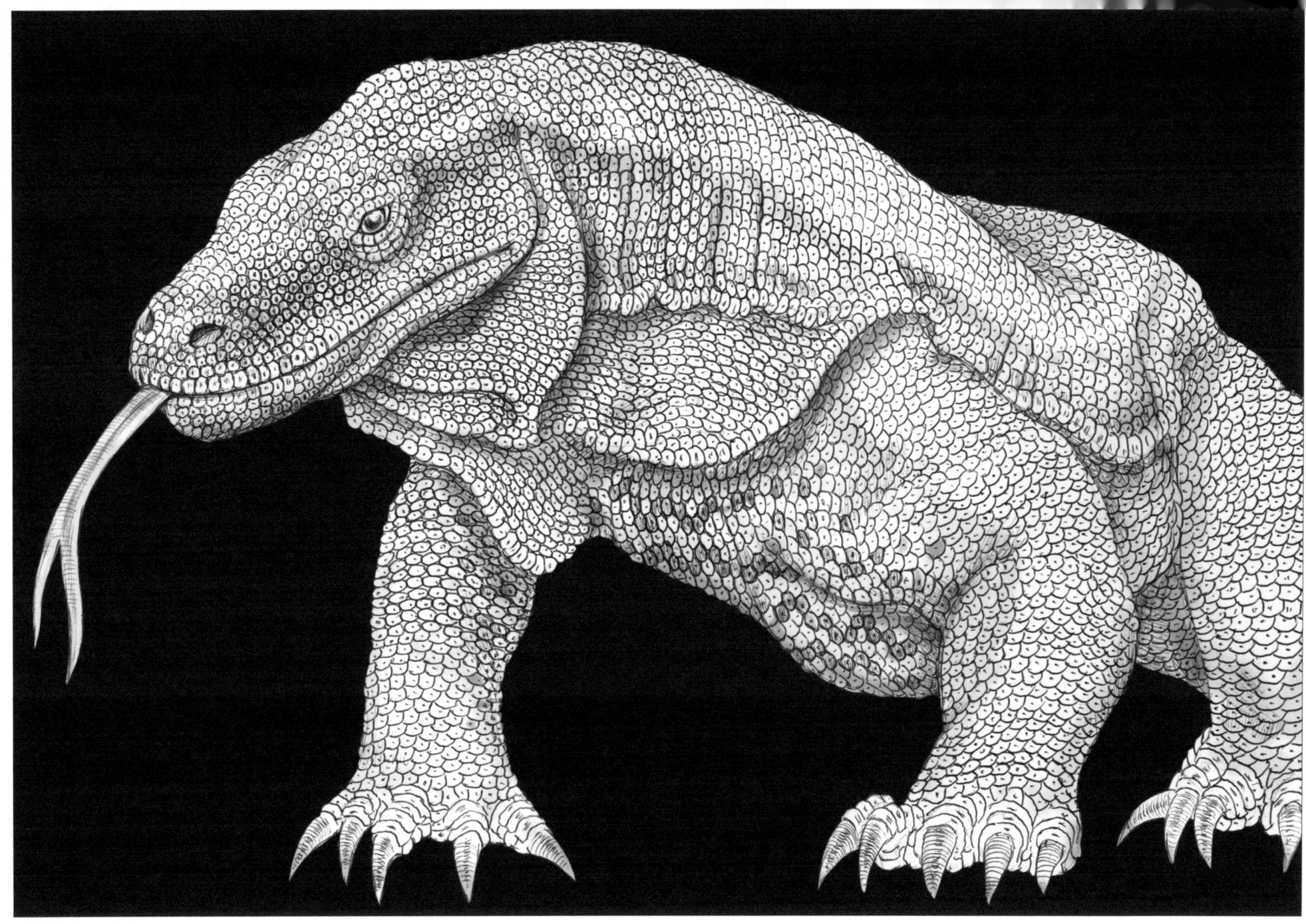

Komodo Dragon

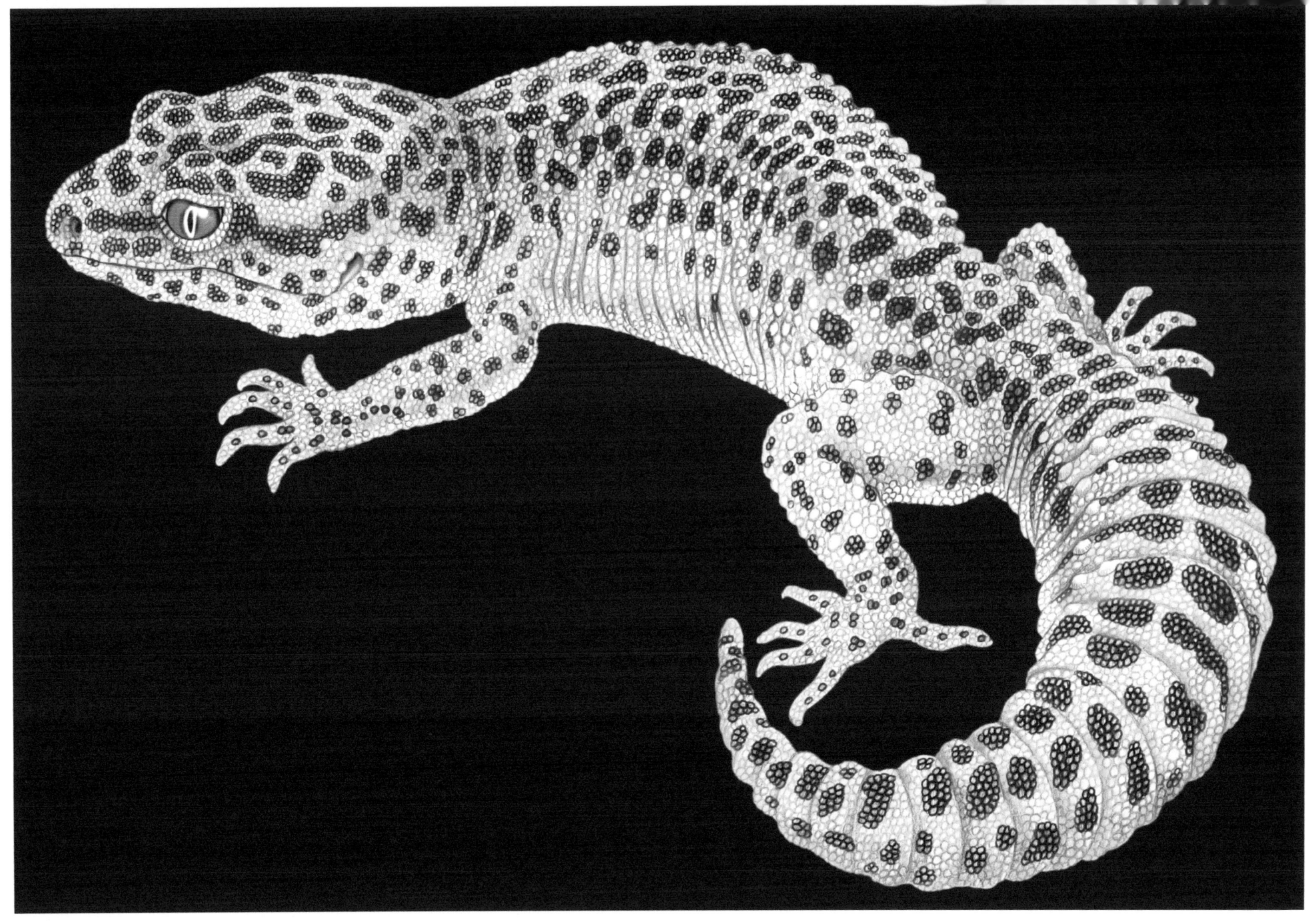

Leopard Gecko

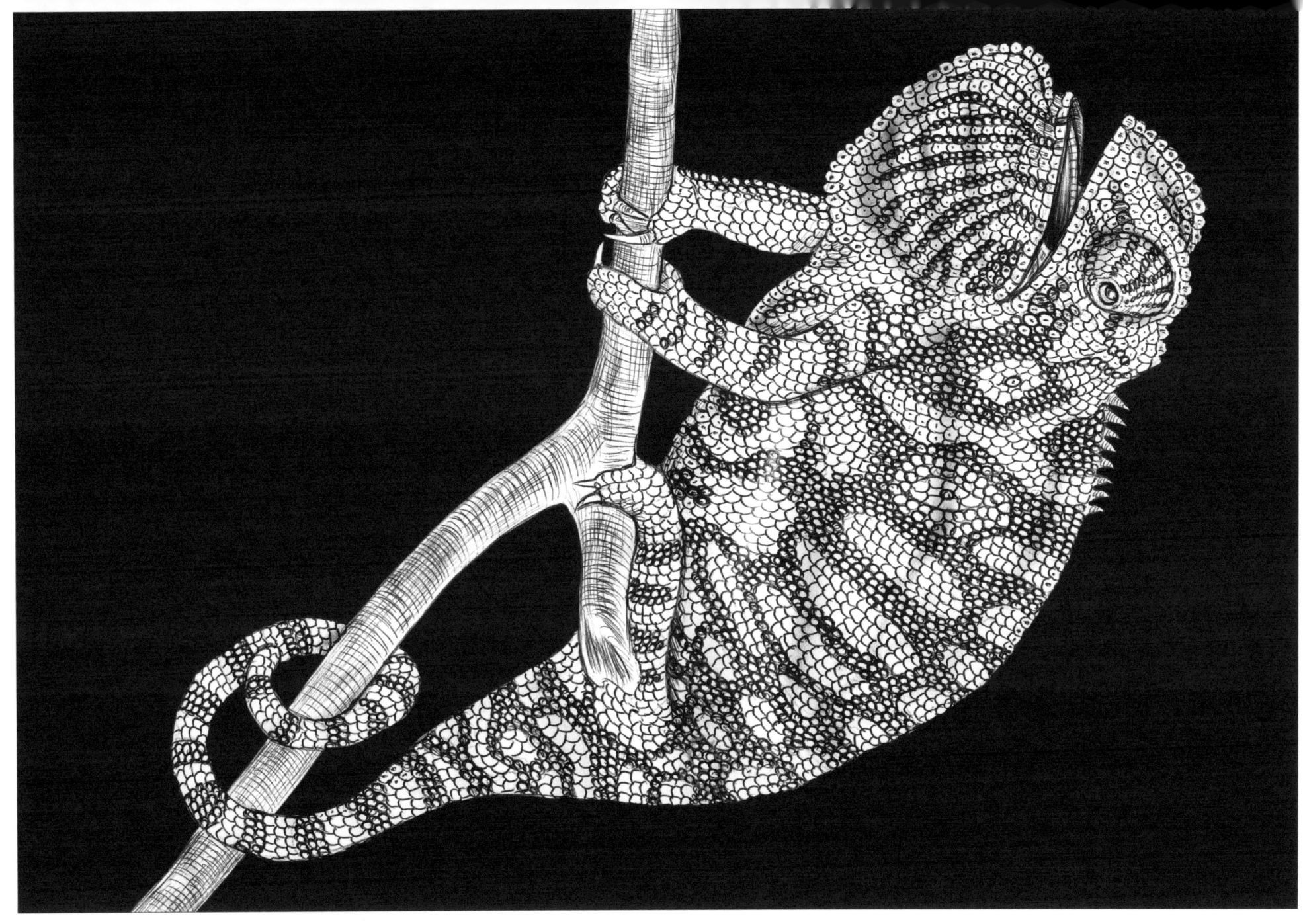

Lesser Chameleon

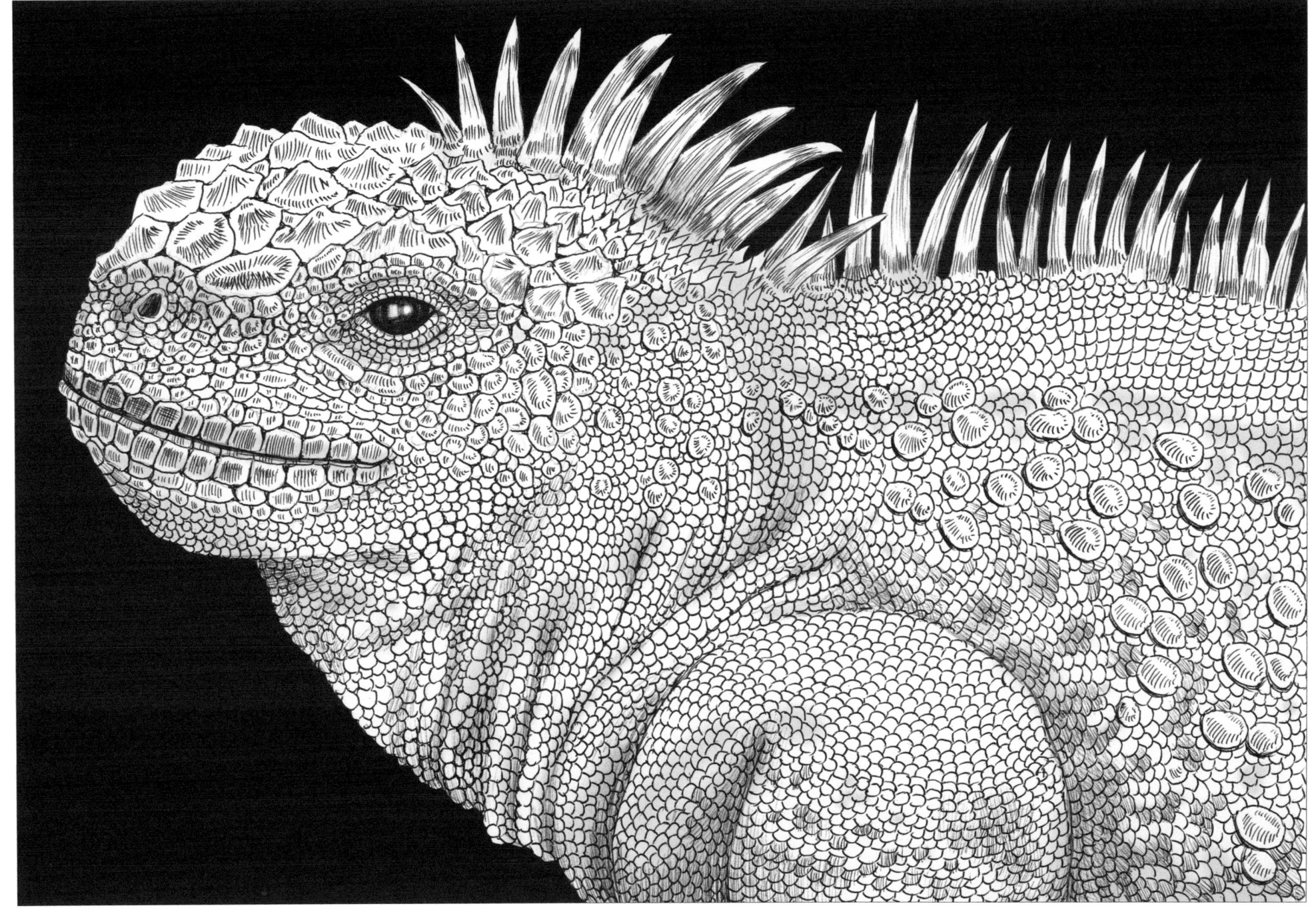

Marine Iguana

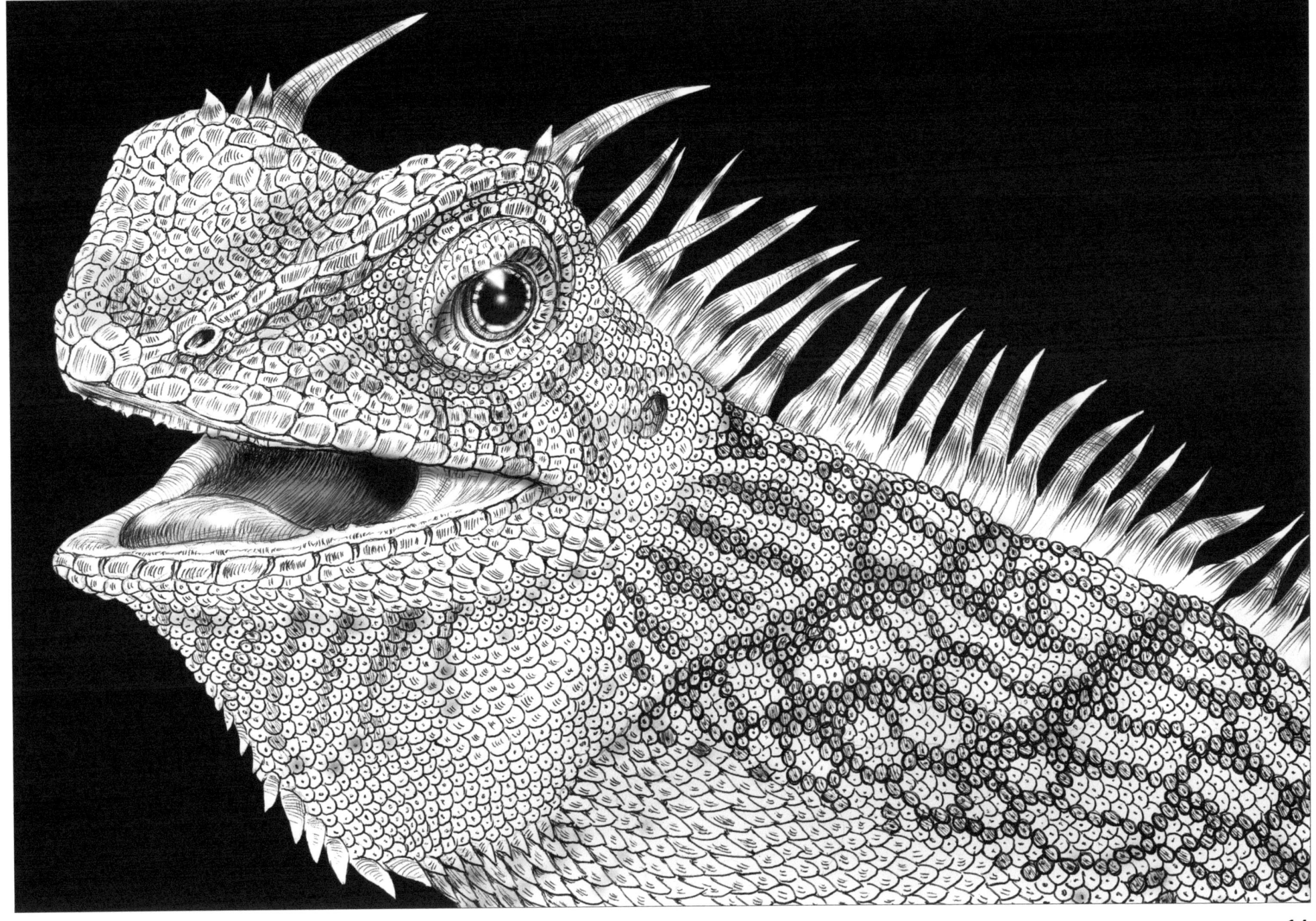

Mountain Horned Lizard

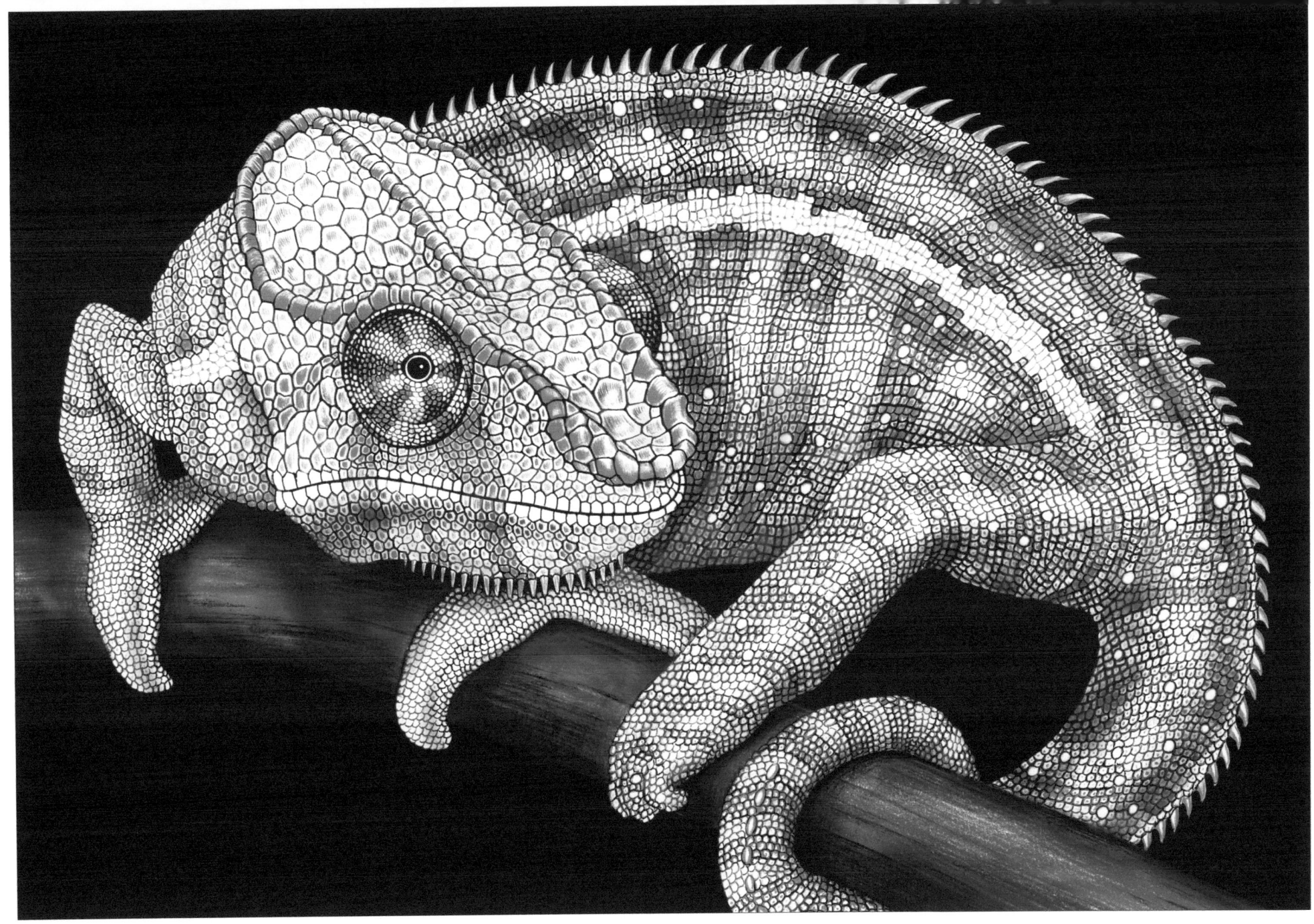

Panther Chameleon

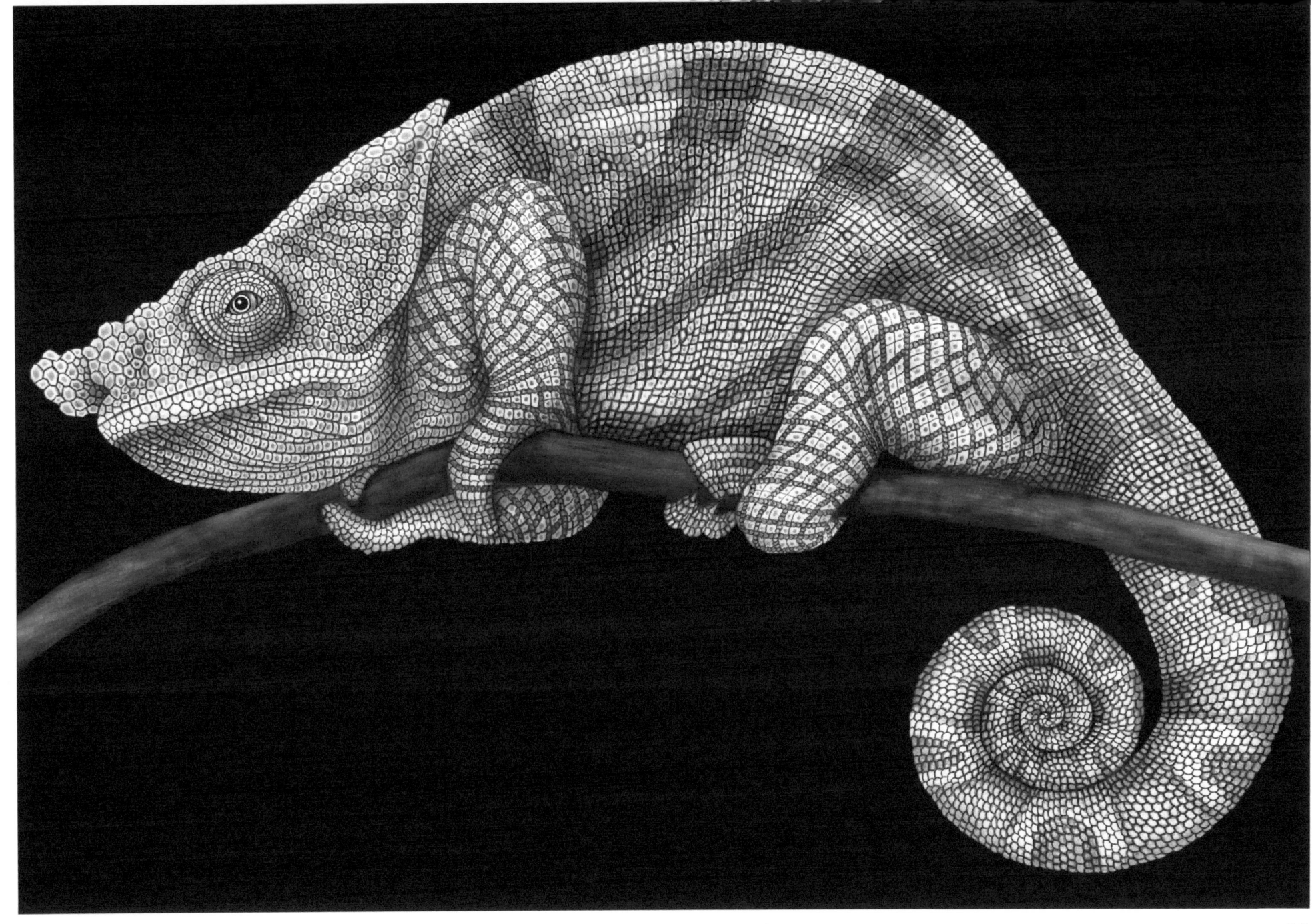

Parsons Chameleon

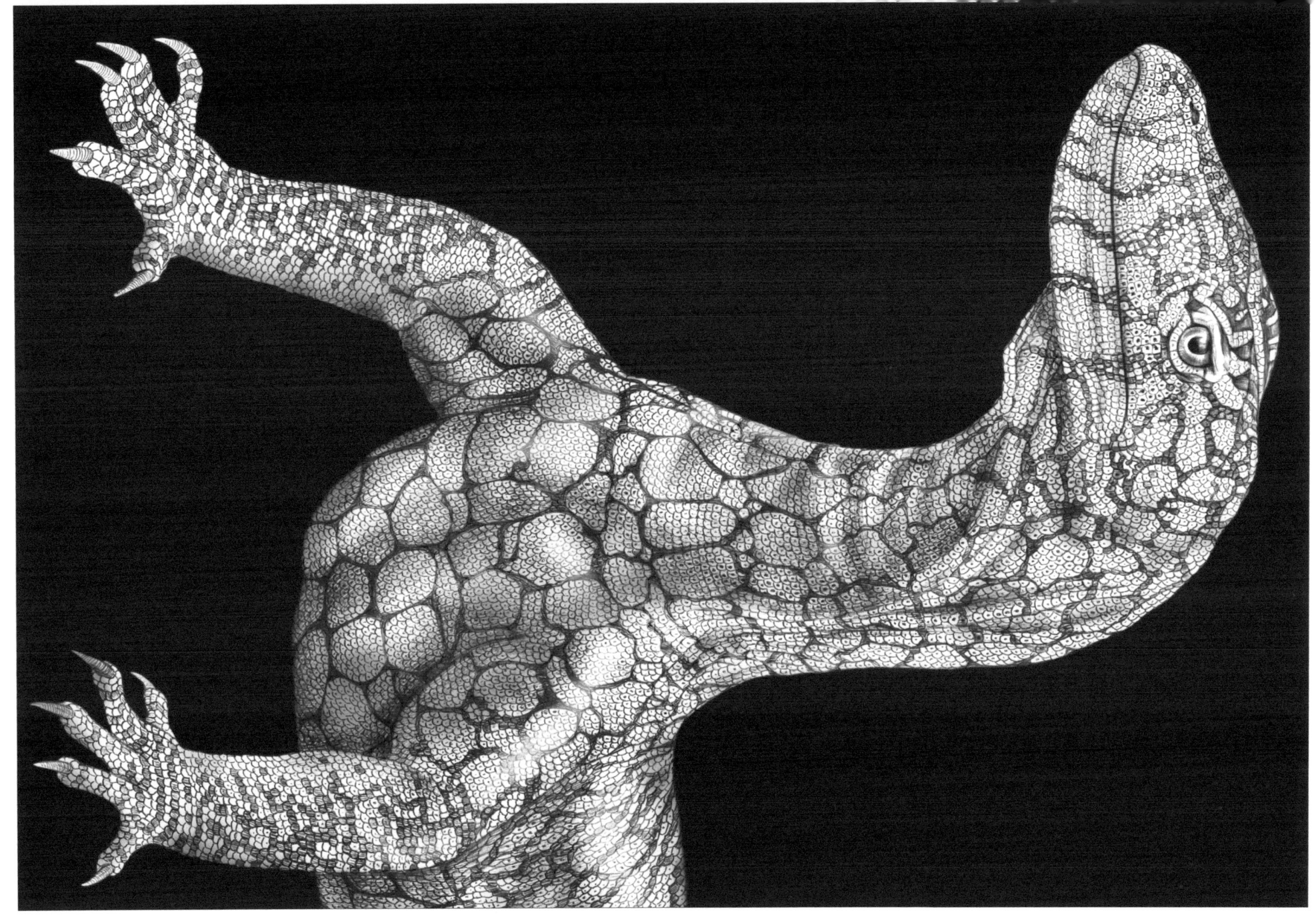

Perentie

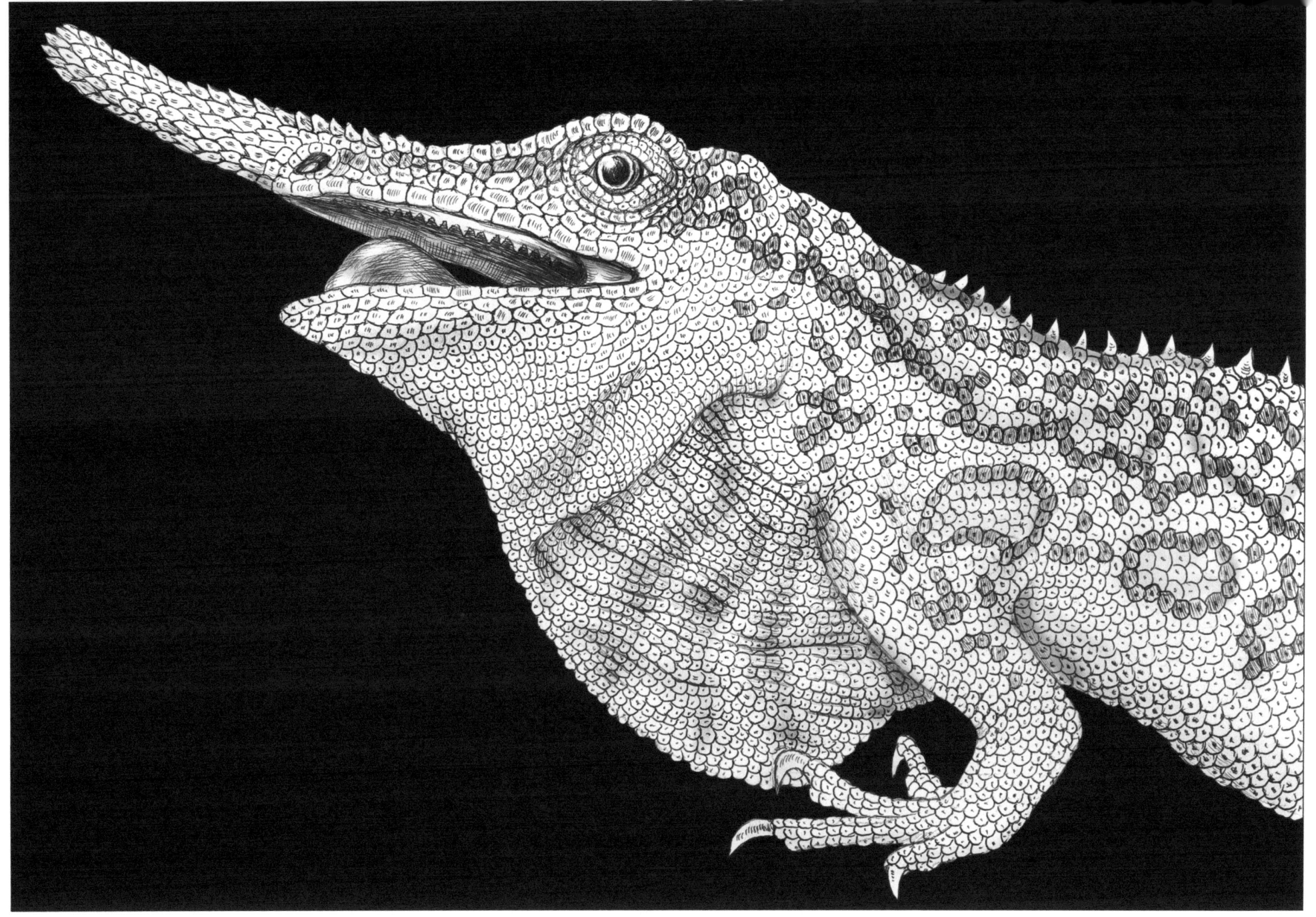

Pinocchio Lizard

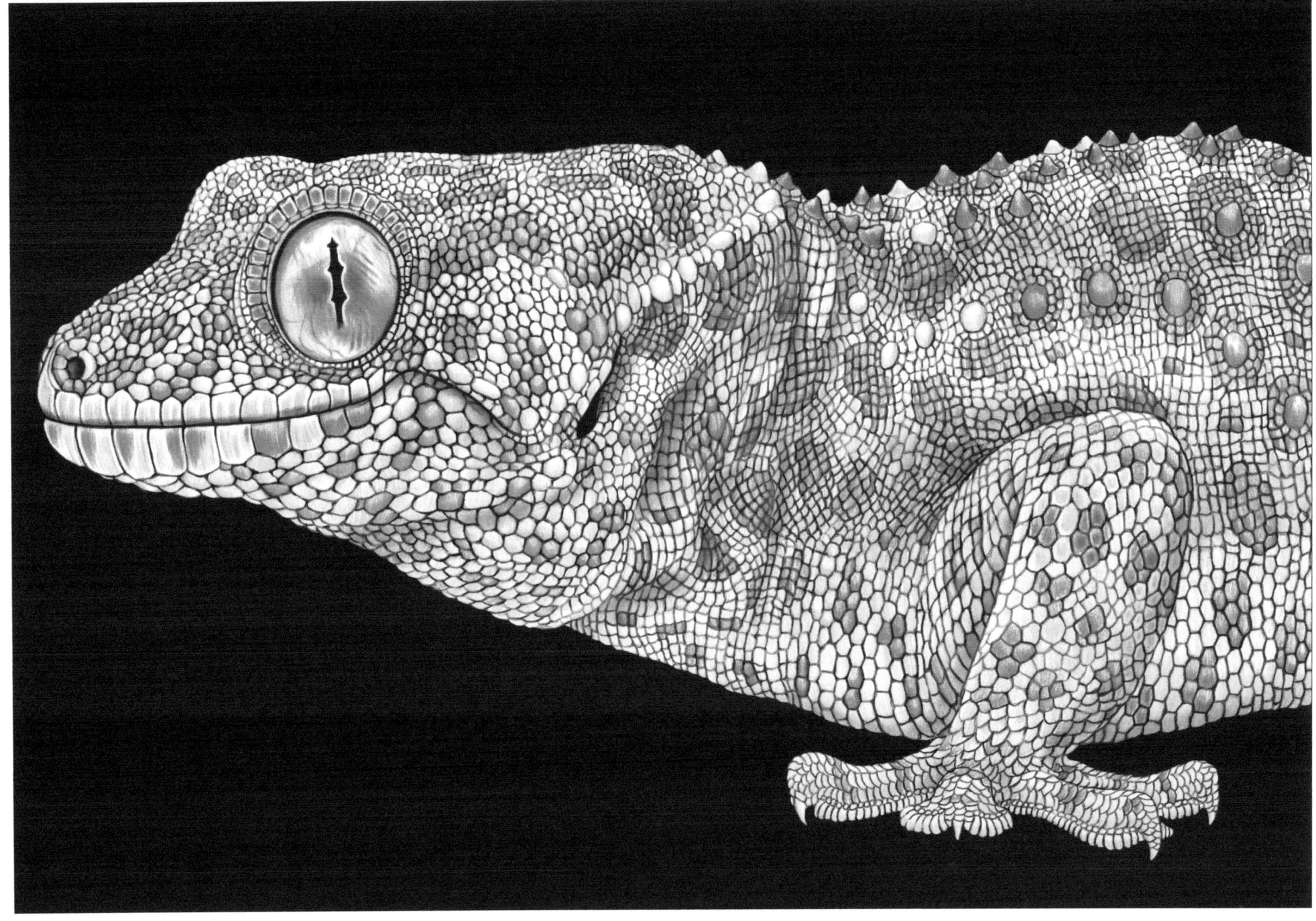
Tokay Gecko

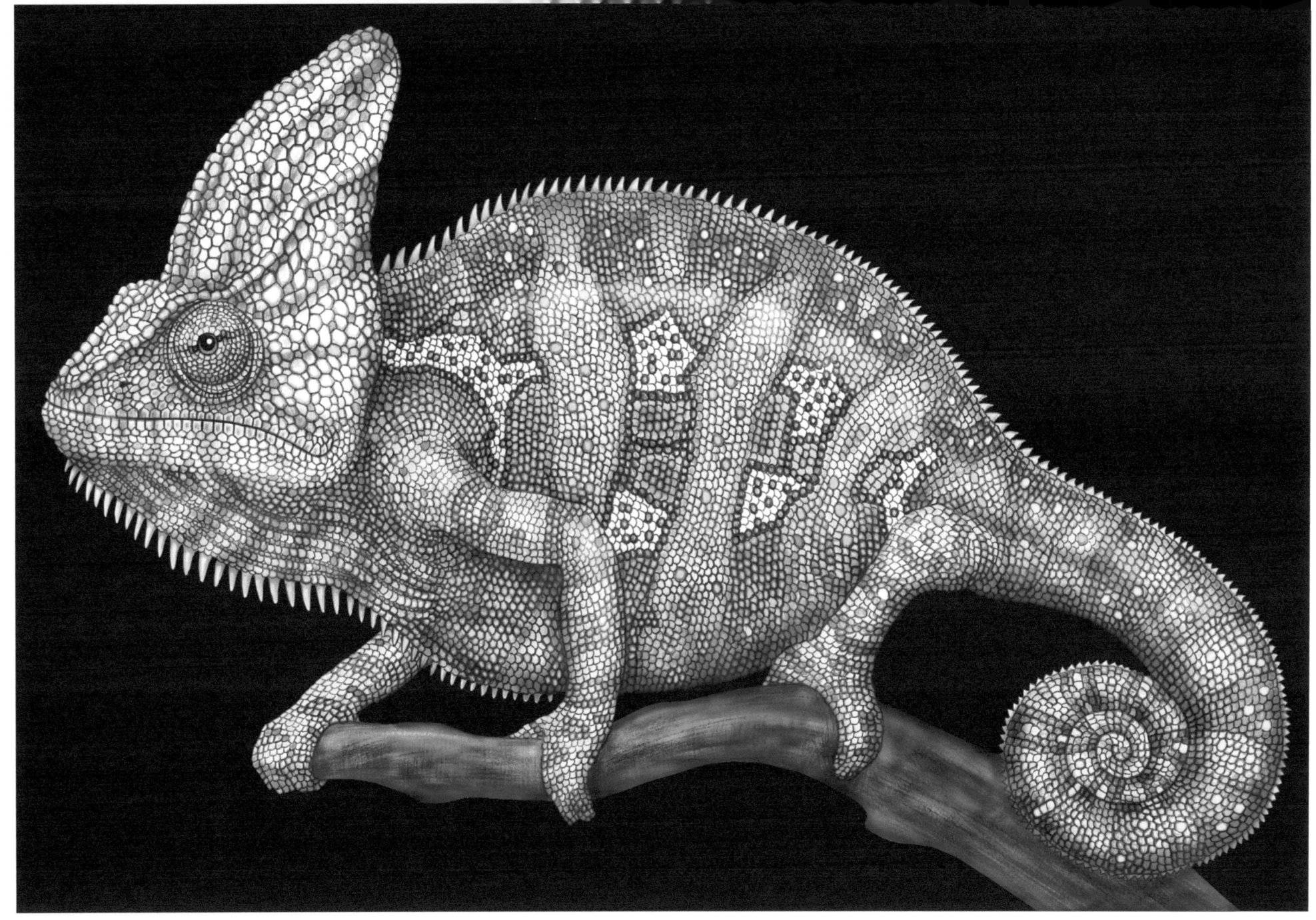
Veiled Chameleon

Tim Jeffs is a New York City based artist and illustrator who has been creating dynamic artwork for over 25 years. Animals are a favorite subject matter of his, along with the complex and intricate details these creatures possess. *"The incredible diversity and complexity of animals has always intrigued me. They offer endless pleasure to look and marvel upon. In every drawing I try to capture the unique quality of each particular animal. I hope you enjoy my perspective, love and admiration of these incredible creatures."*

Visit my website for prints, digital coloring books and coloring lessons:

www.TimJeffsArt.com

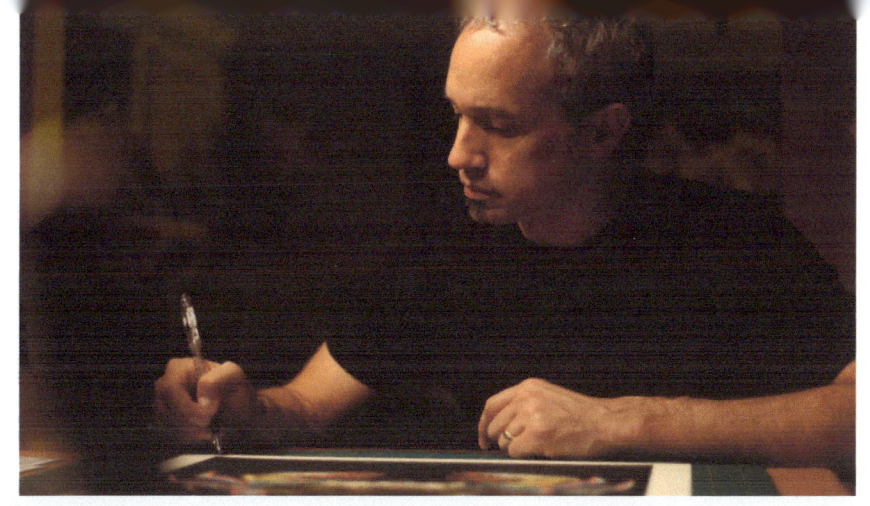

Discover the full line of Tim Jeffs' Published Coloring Books

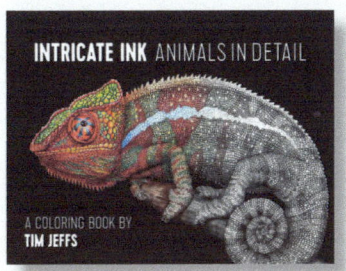 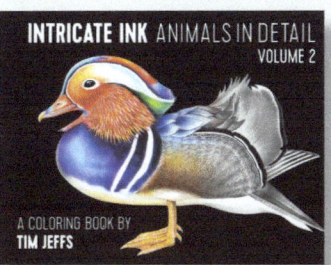 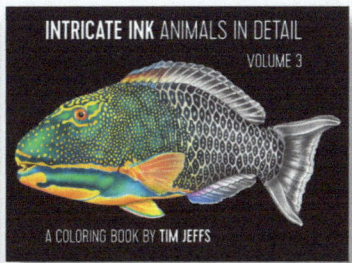 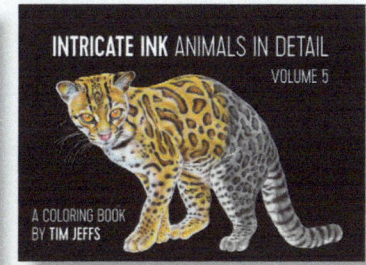 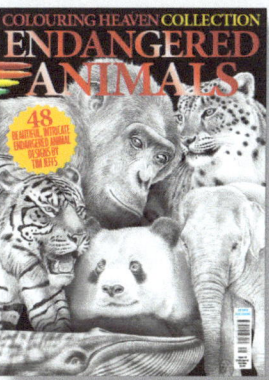

Intricate Ink Animals In Detail Volume 1, 2 3 and 5, and Intricate Animal Drawings Volume 1 and 2 are available at:
Amazon.com
Bookdepository.com

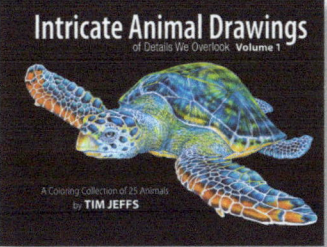 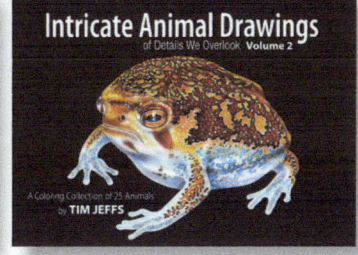

Colouring Heaven Collection Endangered Animals
Available at: Colouringheaven.com

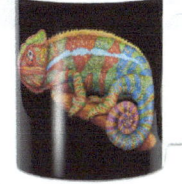

Discover Tim Jeffs' Merchandise

Etsy Shop
www.etsy.com/shop/TimJeffsArt

Society6 Shop
www.society6.com/TimJeffsArt

Redbubble Shop
TimJeffsArt.redbubble.com

TeePublic Shop
https://www.teepublic.com/user/tim-jeffs-art

Discover the full line of Tim Jeffs Digital Coloring Books and Lessons at www.timjeffsart.com

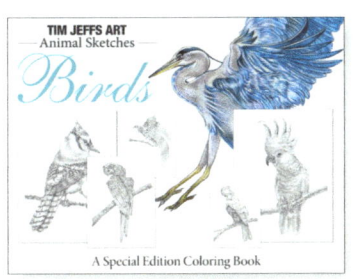
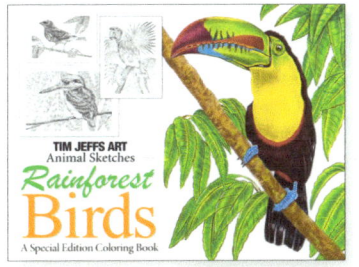
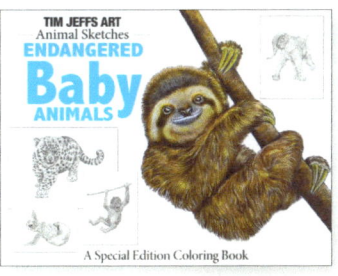
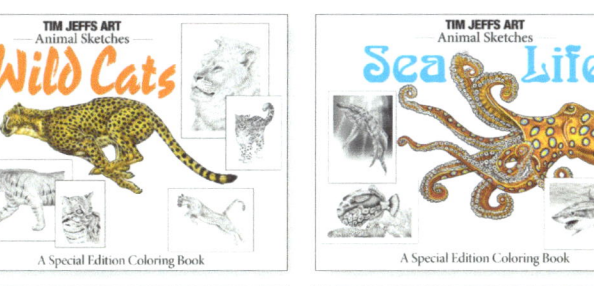

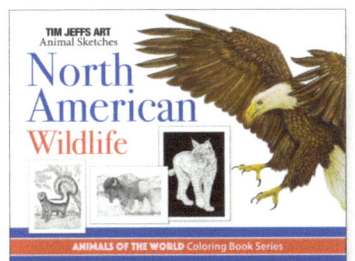
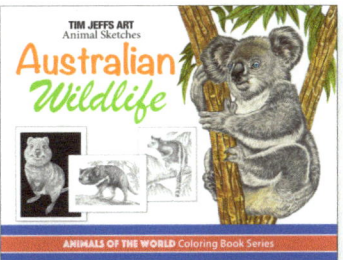
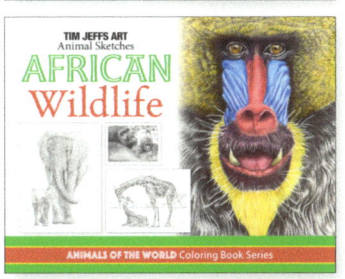
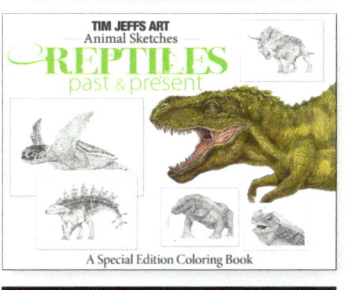
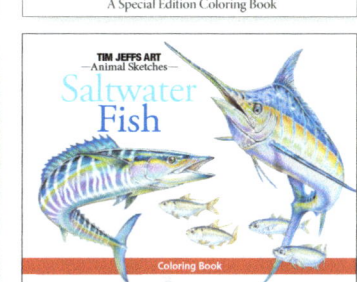

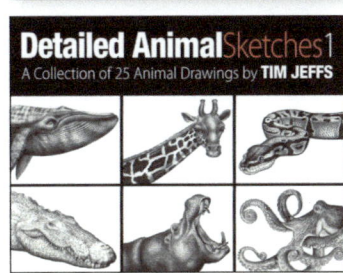
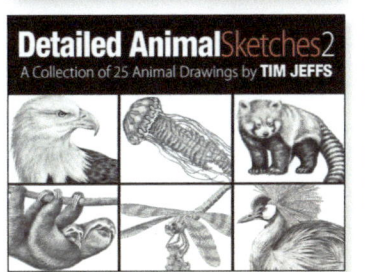
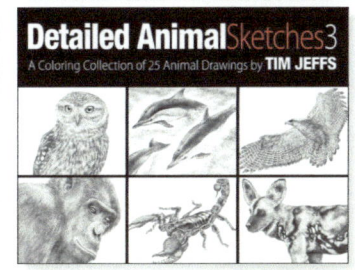
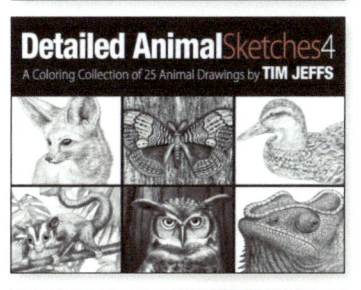
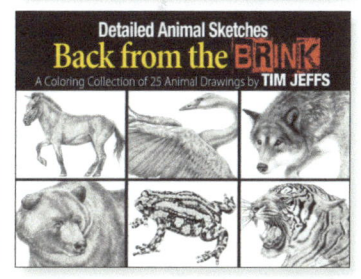

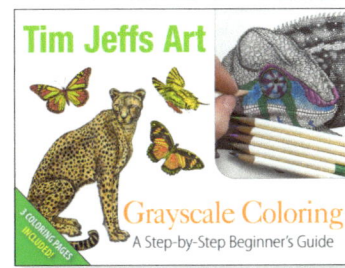
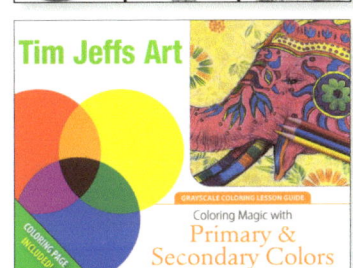
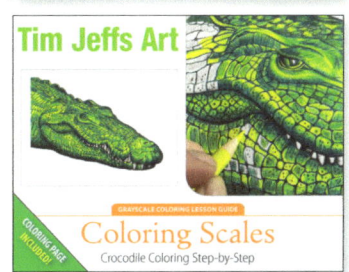
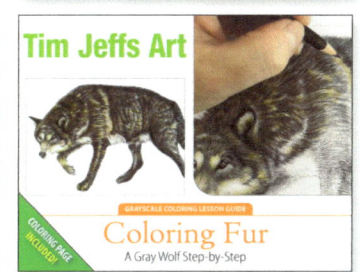
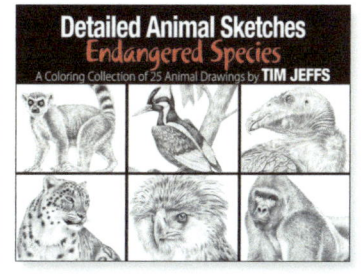

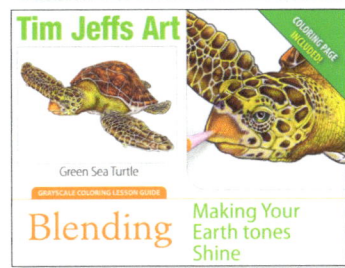
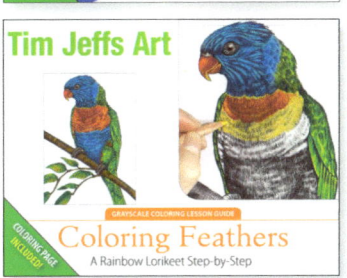
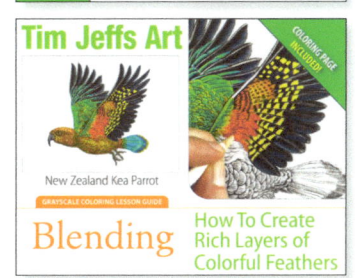
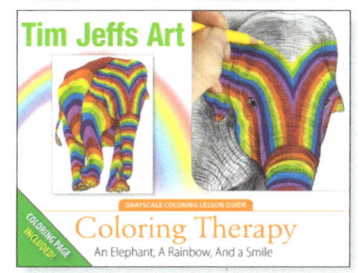
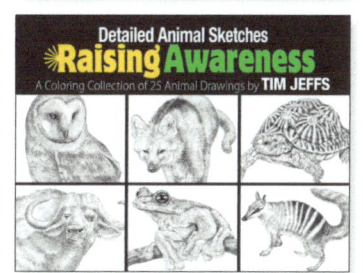

TIM JEFFS ART Online Resources

Share Your Creativity with the World!

Join the ever-expanding coloring group of animal lovers who inspire each other through their colorings of the animals from Tim's books and lessons. With thousands of members from all around the world, Tim's Facebook group "Intricate Ink Coloring Group" is a creative and safe space where everyone is welcome. Jo Warren, the groups all-inspiring administrator will welcome you in with open arms and is there to encourage everyone to just have fun no matter your coloring skill level. Come join, we can't wait to have you as a member! Join Tim's Facebook Coloring Group at:

www.facebook.com/groups/intricateink

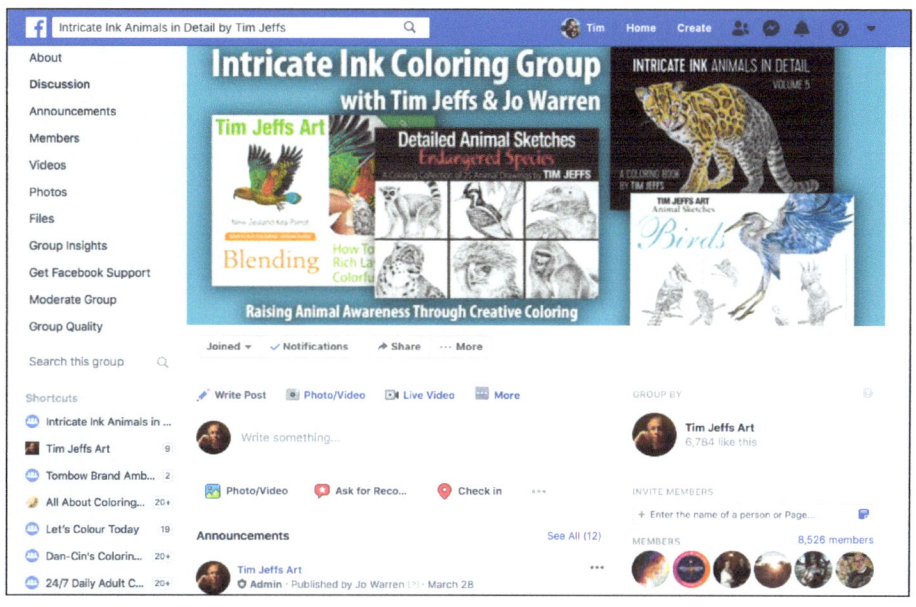

Visit the Home of Tim Jeffs Art

TimJeffsArt.com is my home on the web where I display all of my work and various projects. I hope you can stop by for a visit! You'll find my new shop where signed and unsigned prints of all of my animal drawings are available to purchase, along with the complete library of my digital download coloring books and grayscale coloring lessons. In the conservation section, you can see the projects that I am very proud of. Using my art to preserve wildlife is so important to me.

www.TimJeffsArt.com

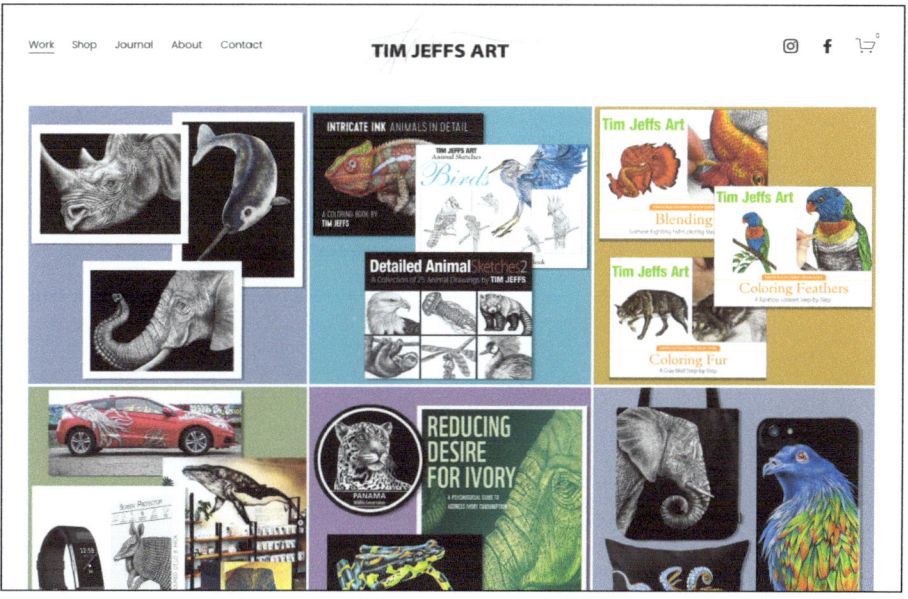

www.ingramcontent.com/pod-product-compliance
Lightning Source LLC
Chambersburg PA
CBHW051221220526
45473CB00003B/1121

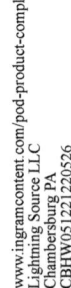